TOM WRIGHT

Tom Wright was Associate Director of Sydney Theatre Company from 2004 to 2012 and has been Artistic Associate at Belvoir Street Theatre since 2015. His plays and translations include *The Lost Echo*, *The Women of Troy*, *The War of the Roses*, *Picnic at Hanging Rock*, *The Real & Imagined History of the Elephant Man*, *The Resistible Rise of Arturo Ui* and *Black Diggers*. He hosts *Breakfast with Papers* at Adelaide Festival and is occasionally heard as a reviewer and commentator on ABC Radio National.

Other Titles in this Series

Mike Bartlett
THE 47TH
ALBION
BULL
GAME
AN INTERVENTION
KING CHARLES III
MIKE BARTLETT PLAYS: TWO
MRS DELGADO
SCANDALTOWN
SNOWFLAKE
VASSA *after* Gorky
WILD

Deborah Bruce
THE DISTANCE
DIXON AND DAUGHTERS
GODCHILD
THE HOUSE THEY GREW UP IN
RAYA
SAME

Chris Bush
THE ASSASSINATION OF KATIE HOPKINS
THE CHANGING ROOM
FAUSTUS: THAT DAMNED WOMAN
HUNGRY
JANE EYRE *after* Brontë
THE LAST NOËL
ROCK/PAPER/SCISSORS
STANDING AT THE SKY'S EDGE
    with Richard Hawley
STEEL

Jez Butterworth
THE FERRYMAN
JERUSALEM
JEZ BUTTERWORTH PLAYS: ONE
JEZ BUTTERWORTH PLAYS: TWO
MOJO
THE NIGHT HERON
PARLOUR SONG
THE RIVER
THE WINTERLING

Anupama Chandrasekhar
DISCONNECT
FREE OUTGOING
WHEN THE CROWS VISIT

Caryl Churchill
BLUE HEART
CHURCHILL PLAYS: THREE
CHURCHILL PLAYS: FOUR
CHURCHILL PLAYS: FIVE
CHURCHILL: SHORTS
CLOUD NINE
DING DONG THE WICKED
A DREAM PLAY *after* Strindberg
DRUNK ENOUGH TO SAY I LOVE YOU?
ESCAPED ALONE
FAR AWAY
GLASS. KILL. BLUEBEARD'S FRIENDS. IMP.
HERE WE GO
HOTEL
ICECREAM
LIGHT SHINING IN BUCKINGHAMSHIRE
LOVE AND INFORMATION
MAD FOREST
A NUMBER
PIGS AND DOGS
SEVEN JEWISH CHILDREN
THE SKRIKER
THIS IS A CHAIR
THYESTES *after* Seneca
TRAPS
WHAT IF IF ONLY

Natasha Gordon
NINE NIGHT

Sam Holcroft
COCKROACH
DANCING BEARS
EDGAR & ANNABEL
A MIRROR
PINK
RULES FOR LIVING
THE WARDROBE
WHILE YOU LIE

Lucy Kirkwood
BEAUTY AND THE BEAST
    with Katie Mitchell
BLOODY WIMMIN
THE CHILDREN
CHIMERICA
HEDDA *after* Ibsen
IT FELT EMPTY WHEN THE HEART WENT AT FIRST BUT IT IS ALRIGHT NOW
LUCY KIRKWOOD PLAYS: ONE
MOSQUITOES
NSFW
RAPTURE
TINDERBOX
THE WELKIN

Suzie Miller
PRIMA FACIE

Winsome Pinnock
LEAVE TAKING
ROCKETS AND BLUE LIGHTS
TAKEN
TITUBA

Jack Thorne
2ND MAY 1997
AFTER LIFE
BUNNY
BURYING YOUR BROTHER IN THE PAVEMENT
A CHRISTMAS CAROL *after* Dickens
THE END OF HISTORY…
HOPE
JACK THORNE PLAYS: ONE
JACK THORNE PLAYS: TWO
JUNKYARD
LET THE RIGHT ONE IN
    after John Ajvide Lindqvist
THE MOTIVE AND THE CUE
MYDIDAE
THE SOLID LIFE OF SUGAR WATER
STACY & FANNY AND FAGGOT
WHEN YOU CURE ME
WHEN WINSTON WENT TO WAR WITH THE WIRELESS
WOYZECK *after* Büchner

debbie tucker green
BORN BAD
DEBBIE TUCKER GREEN PLAYS: ONE
DIRTY BUTTERFLY
EAR FOR EYE
HANG
NUT
A PROFOUNDLY AFFECTIONATE, PASSIONATE DEVOTION TO SOMEONE (– *NOUN*)
RANDOM
STONING MARY
TRADE & GENERATIONS
TRUTH AND RECONCILIATION

Phoebe Waller-Bridge
FLEABAG

Tom Wright

THE REAL & IMAGINED HISTORY OF THE ELEPHANT MAN

NICK HERN BOOKS
London
www.nickhernbooks.co.uk

A Nick Hern Book

The Real & Imagined History of the Elephant Man first published in Great Britain as a paperback original in 2023 by Nick Hern Books Limited, The Glasshouse, 49a Goldhawk Road, London W12 8QP

The Real & Imagined History of the Elephant Man copyright © 2023 Tom Wright

Tom Wright has asserted his right to be identified as the author of this work

Cover artwork: Zak Ford-Williams as Joseph Merrick, photographed by The Other Richard; design.**feast**creative.com

Designed and typeset by Nick Hern Books, London
Printed in Great Britain by Mimeo Ltd, Huntingdon, Cambridgeshire PE29 6XX

A CIP catalogue record for this book is available from the British Library

ISBN 978 1 83904 250 8

CAUTION All rights whatsoever in this play are strictly reserved. Requests to reproduce the text in whole or in part should be addressed to the publisher.

Amateur Performing Rights Applications for performance, including readings and excerpts, in the English language throughout the world by amateurs (including stock companies in the United States of America and Canada) should be made before rehearsals begin to Nick Hern Books, The Glasshouse, 49a Goldhawk Road, London W12 8QP, *fax* +44 (0)20 8735 0250, *e-mail* rights@nickhernbooks.co.uk.

Professional Performing Rights Applications for performance by professionals in any medium and in any language throughout the world should be addressed to Soft Tread Enterprises, Suite B4056, Haymarket Creative, Cnr Ultimo Road and Quay Street, Ultimo, NSW 2007, Australia

No performance of any kind may be given unless a licence has been obtained. Applications should be made before rehearsals begin. Publication of this play does not necessarily indicate its availability for amateur performance.

www.nickhernbooks.co.uk/environmental-policy

Introduction
Tom Wright

This is an attempt to write a theatre-poem about the City and the Body. In the case of Joseph Merrick, the two seem closely linked – Joseph was a product of the industrial Midlands, growing up in the pollution and close confines of Leicester. The architecture was that of terraced housing, brick privies, cigar factories, chimneys, mills, workhouses. And when destitute he was taken to the great metropolis, exhibited in the haze and smog of the East End, another curio in a city that was bulging with excess; the centre of empire, of industry, of science. There are two main characters, in so far as there are characters: there's Joseph himself, glimpsed in twenty fragments of a real and imagined life. A one-off, a prize, an anomaly. And there's London, a big machine, breathing, coughing, spewing smoke and steam as it endlessly churns out simulacra.

*

1888. In the same East End, the Bryant and May match girls were on strike; the use of white phosphorous in their repetitive labour led to 'Phossy Jaw', a disease which caused the mandible to swell and abscess, the mutant growths glowing in the dark. The strike drove many to destitution; women were seen wandering the lanes with what seemed beards of bone and skin extending from their faces. Mass production, big business, disfigurement, difference. Modernity was changing cities, changing bodies. Joseph eked out his days in his cell at the hospital, making his cardboard models of cathedrals, taking tea with aristocrats, while on the other side of Whitechapel Road, women were being found with their innards strewn on the pavement. One of the Ripper murders took place within screaming distance of Joseph's window.

*

The authorised version of Joseph's story comes to us from Frederick Treves, surgeon and gentleman, who discreetly casts himself as Joseph's saviour, interpreter, even his friend. Unfortunately, he never seems to get Joseph's first name right and keeps referring to him as 'John'. For Treves, Joseph is a cipher, a passive patient on which can be inscribed a great man's genius and charity. In the famous 1970s play, Joseph seems to become a parable of gay male coming-out. David Lynch, in the 1980s, fashions the story into an ironic take on high humanism (I am not an animal. I am a human being), casting Joseph as an innocent, trapped in the monstrosity of childhood. Lynch has Joseph's death as an act of trying to imitate a print of a sleeping child on his wall, he curls up as if about to re-enter a womb. It's mawkish and cloying, but there's something about it that rings true. A Peter Pan from the Id, perhaps.

*

In this imagining, Joseph realises he's being killed by kindness. The hospital is both his salvation and his tomb. He knows his world isn't real, he is utterly dependent on his nurses and visitors for any reality. He also knows his body follows a different paradigm to everyone else – it is a shifting thing, a changing shape. It doesn't belong. So he wanders into the big city from which he came, listening to the soot-laden stones and leaves. And there he stands, specimen, statue, tree; nature as something rich and strange. He's not there for our moral edification or as a talisman of difference. He's just himself, and he doesn't have to bear all our weight any more.

The Real & Imagined History of the Elephant Man was first performed at Malthouse Theatre, Melbourne, on 4 August 2017. The cast was as follows:

Paula Arundell
Sophie Ross
Julie Forsyth
Emma J Hawkins
Daniel Monks

Director	Matthew Lutton
Set and Costume Design	Marg Horwell
Lighting Design	Paul Jackson
Composition and Sound Design	Jethro Woodward

The Real & Imagined History of the Elephant Man received its British premiere at Nottingham Playhouse on 16 September 2023. The cast was as follows:

JOSEPH MERRICK	Zak Ford-Williams
MISS FORDHAM AND ENSEMBLE	Annabelle Davis
MRS HIGHFIELD AND ENSEMBLE	Daneka Etchells
NURSE WILLISON AND ENSEMBLE	Nadia Nadarajah
YOUNG MAN AND ENSEMBLE	Killian Thomas Lefevre
JOSEPH'S FATHER AND ENSEMBLE	Tim Pritchett

Director	Stephen Bailey
Set and Costume Designer	Simon Kenny
Lighting Designer	Jai Morjaria
Composer and Sound Designer	Nicola T. Chang
Movement Director	Cathy Waller
Casting Director	Christopher Worrall
Voice and Dialect Coach	Kay Welch
Fight Director	Kiel O'Shea
BSL Consultant	Adam Bassett
Audio Description Consultant	Samuel Brewer
Captioning Consultant	Cara Lawless
Dramatherapist	Nikki Disney
Lighting Associate	Luca Panetta
Sound Associate	Jack Baxter
Costume Supervisor	Emilie Carter
Props Supervisor	Alex Hatton
Production Manager	Andrew Quick
Company Stage Manager	Patricia Davenport
Deputy Stage Manager	Amber Chapell

Assistant Stage Manager	Dan McVey
Captioning and	
* Audio Description Operator*	Eleanor Williams
Personal Assistant	Louise Pearson
Personal Assistant	Evangeline Osbon

BSL Interpreters
Gemma Bamber, Winston Denerley, Emma Dunleavy, Ali Green, Harjit Jagdev, Sue MacLaine, Jude Mahon, Max Marchewicz, Kat Pearson, Tom Pearson

In the in-ear Audio Description, Nadia Nadarajah's lines are voiced by Sophie Allen.

Special thanks to:
Mark Hawes (Director, RTST) , Niamh Cusack, Omari Douglas, Beth Hinton-Lever, Beth Steel, Matthew Xia, Zoe Lack, Nancy Medina, Richard Twyman, Anna Burnett, Poppy Shepherd, Conor Gormally, Francesca Tambellini.

This production is supported by a grant from

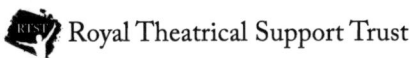 Royal Theatrical Support Trust

Characters

RINGMASTER
JOSEPH
JOSEPH'S FATHER
JOSEPH'S MOTHER
FIRST CIGAR MAKER
SECOND CIGAR MAKER
VOICE FROM ABOVE
YOUNG MAN
FIRST STREET GIRL
SECOND STREET GIRL
THIRD STREET GIRL
FOURTH STREET GIRL
WISE WOMAN
'HER'
'HIM'
WEALTHY LADY
REGISTRAR
NURSE WITH TRAY
FIRST LECTURER
SECOND LECTURER
THIRD LECTURER
FOURTH LECTURER
NURSE WILLISON
FIRST PSYCHIATRIST
SECOND PSYCHIATRIST
NURSE GLYNDON
MATRON
MISS FORDHAM
MRS HIGHFIELD
MORGUE PORTER
NURSE IN CYCLOPS COSTUME
NURSE IN MERMAID COSTUME

Suggested Role Allocations

First Actor
Ringmaster
Second Cigar Maker
Voice from Above
Nurse Glyndon
Second Street Girl
Second Lecturer
Second Psychiatrist
Nurse in Cyclops Costume

Second Actor
Joseph's Father
Young Man
Fourth Street Girl
'Him'
Wealthy Lady
Nurse with Tray
First Lecturer
First Psychiatrist
Matron
Mrs Highfield
Morgue Porter

Third Actor
Joseph's Mother
First Street Girl
Wise Woman
Registrar
Third Lecturer
Nurse Willison

Fourth Actor
First Cigar Maker
Third Street Girl
'Her'
Fourth Lecturer
Miss Fordham
Nurse in Mermaid Costume

Fifth Actor
Joseph Merrick

Note on the Dialogue

A dash (–) at the end of a line indicates one line following quickly on from the previous to the point of interruption at times.

Where lines appears without traditional punctuation it is left to the performer to interpret the rhythm they take.

This text went to press before the end of rehearsals and so may differ slightly from the play as performed.

One: Ringmaster

A woman, late Victorian dress, emerges from the darkness.

RINGMASTER. We are living in desperate times.
    Clouds of black fill the skies
    Casting us all into endless night
    Old certainties are crumbling
    And strange new beliefs
    Have slithered up to crawl upon the earth
    Yes
    Pernicious ideas beget strange forms
    Apes are men
    And men are devils
    Old prophecies warned us
    That signs shall be sent
    The ordained universe
    Would mutate
    That when the legions spring forth
    To call us to account
    They will come from our wombs
    And we shall not know them.
    Listen
    The metropolis hums
    A million souls chew their chops
    Suck their ale
    Snore
    And wail:
    Homo sapiens
    The thinking creature
    But perhaps, perhaps
    Others dwell among us already
    Like us, but not us
    Nephilim
    Hybrids

Mongrel forms
They limp and hobble over the earth
Heads beneath shoulders
Monstrous feet
Perhaps a backbone of eyes
Maybe a malformed twin
Spilling from a ribcage
Multitudes of limbs
Like arachnids they scatter
From the sides of our eyes
Into shadows?
Of course you believe none of this
No
The Nephilim
Live only in our ancient tales
And the nightmares of children
Yes
Very reasonable
Very sensible
Our wise
Enlightened age
No, we have no monsters any more.
Ladies, gentlemen
What if I were to tell you
That I have
In this house
A creature
That fulfils prophecy?
One of the signs
A relic reborn
A throwback
A being so grotesque in form
That it affronts
The very order of nature?
Is it a beast?
Is it a man?
For when you gaze into
The eye
Of this pachyderm

Through the monstrous wart of flesh and bone
When you gaze
Ladies, gentlemen
Into that eye
You may see pain
You may choose to see fear
You may see
Even in that retarded miniscule brain
Knowledge of the Lord
You may
Peer into this malformed eye
And see yourselves.
Ladies, gentlemen,
Examine your souls
Do you need
Truly need
To see the monster
That our age of reason has brought forth?
Have you the fortitude?
If you can enter with a stout heart
A sixpence
A meagre sixpence
Will buy you
An audience with –
Well
I shall let you see for yourselves.

Darkness.

Two: Joseph and His Father

JOSEPH *is a boy. Walking in the fog, searching.*

JOSEPH. Father!
    Father!
    Father!
    Father!

JOSEPH'S FATHER, *drunk, sways into view. Muttering. Gin bottle in hand.*

JOSEPH'S FATHER. This blighted world

JOSEPH. Father
Mother says it is time to come home

JOSEPH'S FATHER. That you Joseph?
Stand up straight
I am tired
You must be
My staff

JOSEPH *keeps his father upright.*

Look at all these mills listen to them
Churn churn churn

JOSEPH. Yes Father

JOSEPH'S FATHER. Look what it has done to us
Churn churn churn
Bolts of cloth all the same
Spoons and forks
All the same
The kettle on the hob in EVERY ONE OF THESE HOUSES
All the same

JOSEPH. Yes Father

JOSEPH'S FATHER. Machines
Big machines
Make everything the same
And we are becoming all the same
Same clothes
Same drink
Same devils
Same sins
Yes?

JOSEPH. Yes Father

JOSEPH'S FATHER. You are not like the others
Are you boy?

JOSEPH. No Father

JOSEPH'S FATHER. You don't know what I speak of
  I saw you in the wash house
  Your beautiful boy skin
  It is dimpling
  And collapsing in itself
  And discolouring
  It catches light like dough
  Waiting the oven
  Like the moon
  And her scars

JOSEPH. Are you angry with me, Father?

JOSEPH'S FATHER. I am a seer
  The future
  Unfolds
  And your future
  My lad
  Is murky murky murky
  You are not right
  You are not the same

JOSEPH. It's just my hip, Da, it will get better.

JOSEPH'S FATHER. No.
  They'll come after you
  Want a piece of you

  Fighting an imaginary assailant.

  Stay away you fiend
  You won't get any more from me!

JOSEPH. Yes Father
  Almost home

JOSEPH'S FATHER. Listen to me
  You will work
  Your limp will not impede you
  And you will earn your way

JOSEPH. Yes Father

JOSEPH'S FATHER. Stop
>Hearken to me
>Your study is to be
>As other boys are
>Do you understand me?

JOSEPH. Yes Father

JOSEPH'S FATHER. Watch them
>Observe them
>Learn
>This is the age of sameness
>This world hates
>Anything different
>We must learn to live among the machines
>They are watching us
>We must be in this world but not of it
>Keep the real you under a bushel
>Yes?
>Well
>Do you follow?

JOSEPH. I think I am too young

JOSEPH'S FATHER. What is this?

JOSEPH. It is our house, Da

JOSEPH'S FATHER. Even the houses are all the same

He sways away.

JOSEPH. Father!
>Come back!

JOSEPH'S FATHER. In the world Joseph!
>But not of it!

>(*Singing.*) In the world but not of it...

He disappears, swaying, singing.

Three: Joseph and His Mother

JOSEPH'S MOTHER. I grew large in the belly
    As mothers do and have done since Eve first bore Cain

JOSEPH. That was me.

JOSEPH'S MOTHER. Yes, you Joseph
    You were growing within
    I could feel you tumble
    And roll
    You would swim
    You would fly

JOSEPH. And you were all around me

JOSEPH'S MOTHER. I suppose so.
    But one day

JOSEPH. A circus came to Leicester

JOSEPH'S MOTHER. A circus came to Leicester
    We heard it before we saw it
    Around the corner it came
    A procession
    A drum-major with a large stick

JOSEPH. It is called a mace

JOSEPH'S MOTHER. Is it?
    You are a one Joseph
    Yes with his mace
    And a bright blue uniform
    And a white hat
    And two white ponies with pink feathers
    From their brows
    And a family of monkeys
    Having tea in a cage
    And a strong man
    In a leopard skin
    And a lion with huge fangs lying on straw
    And bears with ribbons

Dancing to a hurdy-gurdy
And then
From around the corner –
Oh it was large
So big it was like a mountain

JOSEPH. A lumbering mountain

JOSEPH'S MOTHER. As if it had all the time in the world
The largest creature on God's green earth
Ears like sails on a ship
And a long snout
That it used
To catch cornstalks the keeper was tossing

JOSEPH. Was I frightened?

JOSEPH'S MOTHER. You couldn't see.
But I could see
Could see the eye
The tiny eye
In that big big body
That little eye
Was so sad
Sad
And scared
As if a little innocent thing
Was trapped inside
That moving mountain.

JOSEPH. But the heavens opened

JOSEPH'S MOTHER. Oh it poured like the time of Noah
And the strong man
And the simpletons pulling the apes and the bear-gypsy
All scattered
Crying and shouting
And in the panic and the mess
The leviathan
With the little frightened eyes
And the legs like tree trunks
It took afeared

The great skull waved side to side
To see where it might escape
The long snout
Curled up like an Indian serpent
And it came crashing through bearing down on top of me
I was heavy with you
And could not move
And I fell onto the wet stones
And all Leicester screamed
For the massive creature
Was about
To bring the full weight
Down
It reared up on hind legs
And bellowed
Like the angels' trumpets
On the day of judgment
And revelation
A hideous blast
Calling us all to account
And I stared up
In my last moment
And I saw that little eye
Glint
And the two massive legs
Came down
One by my ear,
One by my hip
Pressing my bonnet
Pressing my dress!
I was spared and you were too
The creature backed away
Loped down Humberstone Road
We had been spared
For the Lord's purpose
I do not know what that purpose is
But you were not crushed
By that beast
On that day

And there is a reason
Joseph?
You are being quiet

She holds him, feeling him, checking the growths on his flesh.

Joseph?
What are these
On your skull?

JOSEPH. What happened to the elephant?

Four: Cigar Factory

JOSEPH *and two other children in a cigar works. They cast anxious glances upwards, aware they are under scrutiny. Whispering.*

FIRST CIGAR MAKER. What's wrong Joseph?
Why have you stopped?

JOSEPH. It's my hand
It isn't
You know
Grasping proper

FIRST CIGAR MAKER. Well concentrate
If they're rolled wrong
You get nothing
And we're all in for it
Understand?

JOSEPH. I'm trying
I'm trying
I could do it last week.

Another one falls out of his hands. Another child notices.

SECOND CIGAR MAKER. What's amiss with Joe?

FIRST CIGAR MAKER. I don't know
　His hand see?
　It won't close
　Can't
　You know –
　Grasp

SECOND CIGAR MAKER. That's funny

FIRST CIGAR MAKER. It won't be funny
　If he can't work

　JOSEPH starts to cry.

JOSEPH. My dada will kill me
　Look
　It won't stay in

　He gets up and limps out. They watch him for a moment, then work, quickly, casting anxious glances upwards.

Five: Mother Dies

JOSEPH, *yelling at an upstairs window. As if talking to God.*

JOSEPH. It is me
　It is Joseph
　It is Joseph

VOICE FROM ABOVE. Go yonder Joseph
　You must fend for yourself now

JOSEPH. Is Mother better?

VOICE FROM ABOVE. She is not better Joseph
　You have been told this
　So many times
　She was never going to be better
　You should be joyful
　For she has been freed from this sad

    City of Destruction
    Pray
    Pray
    And live Joseph
    But this is no longer your home
    You are a man now
    And must be a man.

    Pause

JOSEPH. Mother
    Is dead?

    There is no answer.

Six: Beautiful Young Man

A beautiful YOUNG MAN.

JOSEPH *sitting, nowhere to go, drinking from the bottle.*

JOSEPH. What are you gawping at?

YOUNG MAN. I am looking at you.

JOSEPH. A king may look at a cat I suppose.

YOUNG MAN. Quite.

   Pause.

JOSEPH. It started when I was a lad. Crept up on me. These growths. This skin.

YOUNG MAN. And they will grow larger.

JOSEPH. You know that for a fact do you?

YOUNG MAN. I do. They will grow until they are vaster than the rest of you.

JOSEPH. You a doctor, sir?

YOUNG MAN. No. I'm a collector, I suppose.

JOSEPH. Well you can't collect me

YOUNG MAN. Not yet, perhaps.

> Good day, Joseph Merrick. May I proffer a word of advice?
> If you don't want to be collected, stay on the move.
> Otherwise you might put roots down. Become a tree.

JOSEPH. Or a statue in the marketplace

YOUNG MAN. A skeleton in a case. And so on. You are...
not usual. This world is very, very bored with itself. You are
interesting. And interesting things don't just vanish. They are
collected.

He raises his hat and leaves. JOSEPH *stands, in some pain, tosses the bottle aside, and starts to lumber. There is a beauty to his gait that is all his own.*

Seven: Girls in the Street

JOSEPH, *lumbering, in pain, starving.*

Local girls in the mist

One watches him for a while

FIRST STREET GIRL. That's the fifth time you've been down here this afternoon. You lost?

JOSEPH. I know these streets deep in my bones.

SECOND STREET GIRL. Where you going?

JOSEPH. Nowhere.

FIRST STREET GIRL. Well if you've got no business then don't come spying round here with your funny walks, scaring the little ones.

SECOND STREET GIRL. Go on
>Get
>You're drunk
>Can tell by your stumbling
>Oh my God
>Is that your hand, lad?
>Here, you're not a leper are you?

JOSEPH. No
>I am nothing

FIRST STREET GIRL. What is it?

JOSEPH. No one knows the words for it

FIRST STREET GIRL. You're a bit daft aren't you?
>Here
>Come here
>Look at this lad
>Look at his arm

THIRD STREET GIRL. Ooh like it's been twisted
>In a mangle
>And what's that on your head?

JOSEPH. That is my head

They have him hemmed in, he can't keep lumbering.

SECOND STREET GIRL. Here
>Can I touch it?

JOSEPH. No

THIRD STREET GIRL. What else you got wrong with you?

Another girl.

FOURTH STREET GIRL. What's going on here?

FIRST STREET GIRL. A boy
>Says he's just walking
>Walking in big circles
>Round the world

JOSEPH. Feeling faint

FOURTH STREET GIRL. Well you can't stop here
　A gin-stinking tramp

THIRD STREET GIRL. He's not drunk
　He's a cripple
　Look

FOURTH STREET GIRL. What else is wrong
　Besides the hand and the bits coming out of yer head?

JOSEPH. I have skin
　That is a landscape

FOURTH STREET GIRL. A what?

FIRST STREET GIRL. I think he says it's a landscape
　Show us

JOSEPH. No

THIRD STREET GIRL. I'll give you a ha'penny if you let me feel your landscape

JOSEPH. Show me the coin

THIRD STREET GIRL. Here
　Now I can touch you
　Ooh
　My gracious
　Like there's more than one of you
　But the other one's all folded up

FIRST STREET GIRL. You can go home
　Tell your mam
　You have touched a monster

SECOND STREET GIRL. I want to feel it too
　It's good luck isn't it, laying hands on a mooncalf?

JOSEPH. I'm not a freak
　I'm from Leicester too

SECOND STREET GIRL. Feel his skull
　It's like ice

JOSEPH. You want to feel something really different?

SECOND STREET GIRL. Oh my Lord that's disgusting!

JOSEPH. Oh don't stop now
   Here
   Have a good feel
   What about this?

JOSEPH holds one of the girls hands, making her feel him. She screams, the other girls pull her from him. For a moment it's an ugly melee. They eventually are able to run away, screaming insults. He watches them run away.

They are all the same.

Eight: Throat Operation

A sinister figure. She's in a butcher's apron, washing her hands

WISE WOMAN. Approach
   Don't be all timid
   I seen girls in all states
   Don't test me patience
   Come out of the dark
   Now let's get these off you m'dear
   Oof there's a stench
   What you got under there
   Rotting eggs?
   An open sewer?

The WISE WOMAN *reveals* JOSEPH. *Doesn't recoil, just looks.*

What in the name of heaven
Are you?

JOSEPH *tries to speak but just a rasping sound emits.*

Now that, my sweet, don't sound too good.

JOSEPH *produces a scrap of paper. The* WISE WOMAN *reads:*

Haven't you got a way with words?
'You perform certain procedures'
My dear
Whatever I may or may not do
Whatever service to the city I may perform
It is for young ladies
And unless you are –
Are you a lady?
No
Very much male –
Then my field of expertise
Is of no use to you
I suspect

JOSEPH *points at his throat. He writes on the paper.*

How long you think you've got before it
You know?

JOSEPH *makes a movement like a shrug.*

You have my sympathies

JOSEPH *points at her.*

What?
What?
You think I can –
It will kill you
And what do I do
With a dead you?

JOSEPH *tumbles coins into the sinister figure's hands, gestures, as if to say, 'It is all I have in this world.'*

Will anyone come looking for you
If…?

JOSEPH *sort of shakes his head.*

Open up

She pours gin down his gullet.

More of it, you'll need it
I want you shickered

And I want that oesophagus
Nice and ginny

The WISE WOMAN *improvises one of her clamps to wrench* JOSEPH*'s jaw open.* JOSEPH *screams, a reedy, tortured scream. She takes a sharp surgeon's knife on a long handle and moves in. Screams.*

Nine: Sideshow Freak

In the distance, the RINGMASTER, *back to the audience, speaking to the street.*

RINGMASTER.…do you need
Truly need
To see the monster
That our age of reason has brought forth
Have you the fortitude?
If you can enter with a stout heart
A sixpence
A meagre sixpence
Will buy you
An audience with
Well
I shall let you see for yourselves…

A young man and a young woman come forward, drops coins in the RINGMASTER*'s hand. They come on stage, hesitant in the darkness.*

HER. This is giving me the right creeps, this is.

HIM. Now, now
Don't let yourself get spooked
By all that flummery

HER. But why does it have to be so bloomin dark?

HIM. It's atmosphere, innit?

Build up
Don't worry
It'll be some poor bloke crippled
From the wars
With a pumpkin under his shirt
And beeswax on his noggin
It's a just a bit of a laugh

We become aware of JOSEPH, *huddled, a shadow.*

HER. Oh sweet Jesus.
Oh sweet saviour.

HIM. Where are its legs?

RINGMASTER. Stand!

JOSEPH *moves upright.*

HER. Ooh it don't half smell.

HIM. What is that
I mean, all that
Is it bone?
Is it, like, tendons and muscle?
It's like mushrooms after rain
Sproutin' out of a woodpile

HER. Like cauliflowers squeezed into pigskin

HIM. Look at its hand
It's sort of
Normal.

JOSEPH *slumps down again.*

HER. Why do you have to bring me here?
Why do we have to see this?
Can't you take me to the theatre
Like decent fellers do?

HIM. I thought it would be a laugh
But he don't do nothing
Nah come on
I need a pint
I'm all out of sorts.

The RINGMASTER *comes into view, swigging from the gin bottle.*

RINGMASTER. You upset people you do
    You're not like the others
    The Hirsute Lady
    And the Mongols and the Pig-boy
    They
    Play their roles
    But you
    You
    Just make an art form
    Out of
    Loneliness.
    It's over, John.
    This city
    Its streets go two ways
    You twig?
    You work for me
    And I work for you
    But
    You're not working for them
    So now
    I don't work for you.
    Sorry?
    You say something?
    Money?
    There's no money.
    I'll be keeping that
    As compensation.
    What're you going to do
    Fight me?

Ten: Panicking City

He is alone.

He lumbers through the fog, through time, his limp becoming more pronounced. We see his body becoming more and more difficult.

The sound of the body, of the heart.

Three WOMEN *walking in the opposite direction. Each time one of them comes close to* JOSEPH *they stop and stare. The pace builds, the sound of the city, of the panicking body.*

The man silently screams, lost in the fog, a Francis Bacon figure.

Eleven: Taken into Hospital

Two women, a WEALTHY LADY *and the hospital's* REGISTRAR, *watching* JOSEPH, *who is limping in small space.*

WEALTHY LADY. ...from Hell. They found him at Liverpool Street, the mob all around him prodding and pushing like some creature in a menagerie. Screaming banshees, he must have been petrified.

REGISTRAR. Strictly speaking the purpose of a hospital is the treatment of patients, based on the belief (or hope) that some sort of cure is possible and may be effected. A hospital is not a refuge.

WEALTHY LADY. I think in these circumstances the normal rules no longer apply. As I understand it Mr Treves is still searching for some diagnosis of what this poor unfortunate might *be*.

REGISTRAR. There is always an explanation for everything.

WEALTHY LADY. Indeed. Certain Christian souls have an interest in assuaging his suffering. We will cover the expense.

REGISTRAR. That's all very well, but look at him. He cannot be in a ward, hidden behind a curtain forever like some theatrical act waiting his entry. He will be sighted by the other patients, the porters will take bribes and bring gawking members of the public in –

WEALTHY LADY. No, of course, he must be taken aside you might say, we will find some out of the way chamber, perhaps in the attic, or down among the furnaces.

REGISTRAR. Is he capable of speech?

WEALTHY LADY. It would seem not. He is trapped inside his affliction. In a universe all his own.

A NURSE *enters, with a tray and some cleaning equipment.*

NURSE WITH TRAY. You wished to see me ma'am?

REGISTRAR. Yes, please approach. We have a new patient in isolation. Sister, you have some experience with the war wounded?

NURSE WITH TRAY. I have cared for the severely disfigured, yes.

REGISTRAR. This man is likewise of altered shape. His name is Merrick. He is not contagious.

NURSE WITH TRAY. Not at all? Yet he is in isolation?

REGISTRAR. Yes. For reasons of privacy shall we say? Sister, I rely on your sense of duty. And your courage.

NURSE WITH TRAY. These eyes have seen the worst disease can ravage on a body, ma'am. I am sure I can care for Mr Merrick.

The NURSE *goes up to* JOSEPH. *When he stops and stares at her she screams and drops the tray. The* WEALTHY LADY *and* REGISTRAR *look at each other.*

Twelve: Specimen

Sudden bright light, the cool light of science. JOSEPH *stands blinking under scrutiny. He is restless, as if he wants to get down. Three* SCIENTISTS. *Later, a fourth.*

FIRST LECTURER. You will note
  The specimen
  Stands at five foot
  Two and a quarter inches

SECOND LECTURER. The head
  thirty-six inches in circumference

FIRST LECTURER. The neck twenty-three inches

SECOND LECTURER. Note this
  The right wrist
  Twelve inches
  And this the second finger of that hand
  Five inches

FIRST LECTURER. Before we speculate
  On what has caused this distortion
  Note
  Two distinct abnormalities of the skin
  This pliable subcutaneous tissue
  Immediately under the dermis
  It has swollen
  Until its quantity is such
  That it has enabled the skin
  To hang loose from
  Adjacent flesh

  Points to the ribcage.

  See here

  Indicates the lower back.

  And here
  It is draped

It may be waved as a curtain
It hangs in sheets
Pendulous

SECOND LECTURER. These massive pillows of flesh are the first anomaly
But note the second anomaly
In the skin
These ubiquitous buboe-type emanations
Or papillomata
They range from small eruptions
Coarsenings of the surface
To this
Huge sprouting gourds of human substance
Masses caught in a moment of time
As they explode into the space available

FIRST LECTURER. These wart-like structures march in advance parties

SECOND LECTURER. Such as here
On the chest

FIRST LECTURER. Or here over the back of the head

SECOND LECTURER. And note
Between the shoulder blades
Down the lower back and buttocks
They colonise as exuberant growths
In this distinctive dusky purple
Deeply cleft
Fissured

FIRST LECTURER. But the penis
The scrotal sack
Ignorant
Of the perversity happening
In close proximity

SECOND LECTURER. All of this is only to describe
The patient's changing, mutating
Skin and flesh

The more lasting fascination
　　　Resides I dare to suggest
　　　In the skeleton beneath.
　　　This is the third anomaly, the bone
　　　Again
　　　Much of the frame
　　　In here
　　　Is as it should be

FIRST LECTURER. Metamorphosis of the bone
　　　Is confined to the following
　　　The right hand and forearm
　　　Both legs below the knee
　　　Here the bone spouts bosses
　　　Of calcification
　　　Some such as this one
　　　The size of child's fist

SECOND LECTURER. Some such as this one
　　　Like an invertebrate
　　　Seeking to escape
　　　Its osseous prison

THIRD LECTURER. Perhaps it is in response to the malformed bone
　　　That this right arm swells as if a balloon
　　　It is three time the size of the left arm
　　　Every bone in this limb
　　　Excepting the scapula and clavicle
　　　Is pointlessly enlarged
　　　As if a satire
　　　Or burlesque

FIRST LECTURER. This arm
　　　See it can be moved and operated
　　　But the wrist and fingers have fused and melded
　　　Into a claw
　　　Of no use to the patient
　　　It is a jumble
　　　Of bone, skin and
　　　Well, of matter

SECOND LECTURER. And yet the fingernails
>Sitting absurdly on this alien world
>Are perfect
>Unafflicted
>Why?

THIRD LECTURER. See by comparison the hand, arm
>On the left side
>Utterly free
>From any malformation
>Willowy
>Refined
>Delicate and neat
>Like the arm of a young girl

FIRST LECTURER. And the feet
>Both horribly transfigured
>Toes
>Gargantuan
>Parodic

SECOND LECTURER. But the bone's rebellion
>Is most dramatic here
>The skull
>As we have observed
>It is bulbous
>Growing according to no pattern
>Familiar more as fungi perhaps
>Bulge
>Without regularity
>Or predictability of form

FIRST LECTURER. The most prominent landmark
>Of the skull's deformity
>Is this promontory
>On the eyebrow
>Head up please
>But see also
>Here on the right side
>It is as if
>Some idea or

An alternative skull
A second attempt as it were
Is erupting
From a fissure here
Above the ear
A haemorrhage of cartilaginous matter
And bone
So the ear itself
Is folded away
And trapped in a cave

SECOND LECTURER. But on the whole
It is an uncharted continent
This skull
For it is difficult
Perhaps impossible
To discern
Where the skull's limit might begin
And the contortions of skin and flesh end

FIRST LECTURER. And the face
Front door to the person
Forehead
Enormous
Irregular
Massive
Setting the eyes deep in the head
The right zygomatic
Is at least four inches thick
Like a rock lodged over the upper jaw
It has thrust the hard palate
Forward and down
Which has evicted the nose and mouth to the left
Open your mouth please
Thank you
If you observe
This scar here

SECOND LECTURER. Clearly some growth or redundant tissue

Has been removed in surgery
At some point

FIRST LECTURER. But see here
This side of the face
Turn your head
Thank you
This portion of the jaw
The eyelid
Again
Note this, the left ear
Perfect
As God designed
But the right ear?
Vanished as we have noted
Swallowed by a skin
In rebellion with itself

SECOND LECTURER. Lower mandible:
Familiar, recognisable, normal.

THIRD LECTURER. What does normal mean here?

SECOND LECTURER. Clearly normal means
As the Creator designed
How you and I appear
According to the pattern ordained by nature

FOURTH LECTURER. Perhaps this is the wrong way
To think of this body
Or any body
Perhaps terms such as
Skin
Bone
Flesh
Are meaningless here
Perhaps we need
New words

SECOND LECTURER. New words?
Ignoring the oddness of form
What in the end

Is truly new
About this being?

FIRST LECTURER. It has no rules
No one has charted it before

THIRD LECTURER. This *is* a body
A recognisable body
But a body at war with itself
A body declining to be limited
To know where it must cease
This body
Like a species without restraint
On a desert isle
It will
Keep going
Sprout
Insist
Burgeon
Until
One assumes
The weight will be so great that
The entire edifice
Collapses into the dust.

FIRST LECTURER. So
What is to be done?

SECOND LECTURER. Hypothesis:
A disorder of chemicals
Swirl in the bloodstream,
Will you stand still please
You are most distracting
And perhaps a chemical compound of some description
might enable resistance to invasion across the map of the
skin, so to speak
Prevent these fantastical growths
Bring the body back into discipline?

FIRST LECTURER. My counsel would be
A range of prostheses and altering devices

Casts, splints, and newly designed implements
That might guide and correct the skeletal disorders
I am assuming here
That the surface afflictions are in some way related to the inner malignancy

SECOND LECTURER. We should not rule out surgery of course
The removal of the great folds of skin
Shaving and rasping at the build-ups of calcium salts
We could saw off the bone spurs
Break and re-set the feet perhaps

FIRST LECTURER. But we are far far up the Nile here
Deep in a dark continent
We are at that point
Where we must concede
We do not know what to do

SECOND LECTURER. But surely
We cannot do nothing
Something must be done

FOURTH LECTURER. Why?

FIRST LECTURER. Do you really think this
Should be simply
Left as it is?

Thirteen: My Name is Joseph

Warm, domestic light.

JOSEPH *being washed by a* NURSE.

NURSE WILLISON. But of course him
Don't understand that
That's what I says to him
You don't understand things Mr Treves
Because you aren't the one

Down here
With the sponge in your hand
I'm the one who touches him
Every day
And I says
We all thought his stench
Was one the symptoms
Didn't we?
And it turned out
He don't stink at all
It's just that no one ever washed you
And now I bathe you
Every day
You're like a little rose garden down here
Our little posy in the cellar
And I says
This is the thing
I says
We don't know what is actually
The problem
And what is just
Caused by the problem
You know what I mean?
There's you John
And then there's
Whatever's wrong with you
And then there's us
And how we know you
And there are a few of us
(Well, there's me)
What reckons there's a lot less wrong than the gentlemen upstairs
Seem to think
I mean
If the stink weren't caused by you
What else are we assuming about you
That isn't there
You know what I'm saying?
No one seems –

JOSEPH. Joseph

NURSE WILLISON. What's that?

JOSEPH. My name is Joseph

NURSE WILLISON. Did you just say
My name is Joseph?

JOSEPH. Yes.

NURSE WILLISON. That's *yes* isn't it?

JOSEPH. Yes

NURSE WILLISON. So you understand me?

JOSEPH. Very well.

Pause while she absorbs this.

NURSE WILLISON. You might have told me!
I've been unburdening my soul to you these last weeks!
I told you all about me mum and the
You know, problems, we were having
And about what
That bloody surgeon does with his hands
When he gets me alone
And about Matron's little issue with the

Gestures drinking.

Right
You have to forget everything
I have told you
You understand what I'm saying
You forget

JOSEPH. I understand
Nurse
You can rely on my discretion.

NURSE WILLISON. Discretion
There's a word.

Pause.

How many fingers am I holding up?

JOSEPH. Four.
   Now eight.

NURSE WILLISON. Well blow me down.

JOSEPH. Your name is Agnes.

NURSE WILLISON. It is

JOSEPH. And mine is Joseph
   Not John
   I would like the doctors to call me
   Mr Merrick
   It seems only polite
   But you Agnes
   Can call me Joseph.

NURSE WILLISON. You know
   Everyone here
   Thinks you are
   Mentally retarded

JOSEPH. I don't know

NURSE WILLISON. It means
   Like a child
   Or unable to think
   Or unable to think things through

JOSEPH. I know what the word *means*
   I don't
   Understand it

NURSE WILLISON. You don't understand it?

JOSEPH. I have been in Hell
   I know nothing of the world
   I do not know
   If I am mad
   Or sane
   I have no
   Comparison.

NURSE WILLISON. Was that *I have no comparison*?

JOSEPH. In my mind
   I am a gentleman
   And in this world
   I am...

NURSE WILLISON. Oo hoo
   This world
   You don't want to know about this world

JOSEPH. Yes
   I do
   Where else do I live?

Fourteen: Word Association

JOSEPH *is sitting. Two well-dressed* WOMEN *sit opposite him. One writing in a notebook. One drinking tea.*

FIRST PSYCHIATRIST. And you merely chose
   Not to speak?

JOSEPH. People ceased speaking to me
   So I had less and less to say in return

FIRST PSYCHIATRIST. And now you have voyaged back to the world of language?

JOSEPH. After a fashion

SECOND PSYCHIATRIST. Is there anything you would like to ask us
   Mr Merrick?

JOSEPH. Yes
   It is kind of you to visit
   But who are you?

FIRST PSYCHIATRIST. Were you not told?
   I do apologise
   We are from another institution
   If you like

SECOND PSYCHIATRIST. The Association of Medical Officers of Asylums and Hospitals for the Insane

JOSEPH. Am I insane?

FIRST PSYCHIATRIST. I would like to try a little game Mr Merrick

JOSEPH. A parlour game?

FIRST PSYCHIATRIST. A sort of parlour game
You simply calm your mind
And I say a word
And without pondering the word
You just say a word in return
The first one that leaps into the mind
Would you care to play this little game with me?

JOSEPH. I am in your hands.

FIRST PSYCHIATRIST. Protect?

JOSEPH. Nothing

FIRST PSYCHIATRIST. Task?

JOSEPH. Elephant

FIRST PSYCHIATRIST. Slip?

JOSEPH. Hip

FIRST PSYCHIATRIST. Drop?

JOSEPH. Snow

FIRST PSYCHIATRIST. Snake?

JOSEPH. Temptation.

FIRST PSYCHIATRIST. Award?

JOSEPH. Hospital

FIRST PSYCHIATRIST. Achieve?

JOSEPH. Fail

FIRST PSYCHIATRIST. Bad?

JOSEPH. Air

FIRST PSYCHIATRIST. Blood?

JOSEPH. Stone.
　Believe.
　True.
　Self.

FIRST PSYCHIATRIST. Mr Merrick
　You must let me speak the words
　So the mind is free to –

JOSEPH. Polite
　Handsome
　Free
　Desirable
　Delicate
　Safe
　Attractive
　Invisible

FIRST PSYCHIATRIST. Mr Merrick
　This technique only works if –

JOSEPH. Within
　Cocoon
　Nervous
　Dormant
　World
　Awake
　Prison
　Ribcage
　Fist
　Gasping
　Government
　Mother
　Cell
　Skull
　Police
　Skin
　Architecture

Suffocate
Suck
Punch
Shit
Soldier
Invisible

FIRST PSYCHIATRIST. Are you getting all these?

SECOND PSYCHIATRIST. No I can't keep up

JOSEPH. Squirm
Scare
Eat
Devour
Complicit
Destroy
Samson
Hatred
Consume
Judgment
Teeth
Claw
Bite
Chew
Vengeance
Jericho
Mother
Skin
Bone
Monster

He is getting worked up. NURSE WILLISON *comes in.*

NURSE WILLISON. Joseph. Joseph.
You can stop now
You can stop.

JOSEPH. Cut
Burn
Bone
Moan

Mine
Fire
Fall
Chains
Pain

NURSE WILLISON. Joseph, stop
Stop stop

JOSEPH. Knife
Dark
Mad
Press
Hate
Kill
No
No
No
No
No
No
No
No

The PSYCHIATRISTS *stand, watching.*

Is that the sort of thing you had in mind?

Fifteen: Miss Fordham

The courtyard of the hospital. The stars above. Eternity.

JOSEPH *and his* NURSES.

NURSE WILLISON. I've set a chair up for you
Here in the courtyard

NURSE GLYNDON. Look up

JOSEPH. The creature in the cage

Sees the same stars
As the bird of the field

NURSE GLYNDON. Is that
Browning?

JOSEPH. No

NURSE GLYNDON. I don't know
Arnold?

Who wrote it?

JOSEPH. I did.

A young girl, well dressed, is led to another chair by MATRON.

MATRON. Joseph, this is Miss Hazel Fordham.
Miss Fordham, may I introduce you to Mr Joseph Merrick.

MISS FORDHAM *curtsies*.

MISS FORDHAM. It is a pleasure, sir.

JOSEPH (*awkwardly standing and attempting to bow*). The honour is mine, Miss Fordham.

They resume their seats. Awkward pause.

MISS FORDHAM. The air in the evening
When it cools
The scent changes
Does it not?

JOSEPH. Oh
Yes.

MISS FORDHAM. A million braziers
Coal grit smoke
The dung of the streets swept into corners
There

(*Sniffing the breeze*.) Stale beer

The clotted blood of the slaughterhouses
Spices
From the ships at Limehouse

You are most fortunate
Mr Merrick
To live here
Away from all that
All that vileness

JOSEPH. I suppose I am

MATRON *comes forward, puts a blanket over* MISS FORDHAM.

Are you cold
Miss Fordham?

MISS FORDHAM. No
But thank you for your concern
My medicine
Makes me convulse
On occasions

JOSEPH. Forgive me
I did not realise
You were a patient.

MISS FORDHAM. I have had fevers
They cause my brain to distend
Under my skull-shell
I will not last to Michaelmas

JOSEPH. I am truly sorry to hear that
Miss Fordham.

MISS FORDHAM. I will never leave this hospital
I keep this smile on my cheeks
See this smile
Can you see it, Mr Merrick?
It is a mask
I have crafted it
Are they looking at us?

JOSEPH. Who?

MISS FORDHAM. Matron
The nurses

JOSEPH. Yes

MISS FORDHAM. The smile is for them
  I am trapped here
  And I am utterly at their mercy
  I must not let them think
  I am unhappy

JOSEPH. Are you unhappy?

MISS FORDHAM (*smiling sweetly*). Unbearably
  If you are difficult
  They get at you

NURSE GLYNDON (*reentering*). And how are you two going?

JOSEPH. Splendidly.

  NURSE *wanders off*.

MISS FORDHAM. I am going to leave here in a pine box
  So I must
  Smile

JOSEPH. Don't you have anyone –

MISS FORDHAM. In the real world?
  There are people
  But I have been here so long
  They must have forgotten I am alive
  I do not care
  In a way
  I am free

JOSEPH. You do not sound free

MISS FORDHAM. Free from having to be anything else
  I am just an illness
  A problem
  That others must solve
  I have stopped caring
  I let them care

JOSEPH. Care you
  To death, Miss Fordham?

MISS FORDHAM. And beyond too

JOSEPH. I think I can remember a beyond

MISS FORDHAM. When things were in their place

JOSEPH. Every night
 From in here
 I listen to the world
 As it erupts out there,
 Beyond the walls

MISS FORDHAM. It is merely the noise
 Of the great city
 Mr Merrick

JOSEPH. But don't you ever wish
 To escape
 Just for a day, to be in that great city?

MISS FORDHAM. It is the same as this hospital
 There are great folk and there are lowly
 Children are born
 Bodies die
 There is nothing else
 This is all there is

JOSEPH. No,
 I beg to differ
 This is a false town
 And out there
 Is real
 For all the pain

MISS FORDHAM. Well
 Why not escape?
 Yes, go

 She laughs as if JOSEPH *has made a joke.*

JOSEPH. What?
 Just walk into the world?
 Me?

MISS FORDHAM. Yes
    Do not leave here in a pine-wood case
    Shamble out
    And disappear

JOSEPH. But Miss Fordham
    That is absurd
    Can you not see me
    Can you not see
    What I am?

MISS FORDHAM. Oh Mr Merrick
    My fevers
    Have taken that sense from me.
    I am completely blind.

    MATRON *comes forward again.*

MATRON. That is your time Miss Fordham
    Too much of this cold air
    Remember what Doctor said

MISS FORDHAM. Of course Matron
    Yes

JOSEPH. Can she not stay a few moments longer Matron?

MATRON. No Mr Merrick
    I think we know what is best
    Don't you?

    MISS FORDHAM *curtsies, smiling sweetly, and is taken.*
    JOSEPH *and the* NURSE *sit for a while.*

JOSEPH. What is a hospital, Agnes?

NURSE WILLISON. I don't understand, it's as plain as the nose on your face.
    Oh sorry
    Could have chosen a better
    Um

JOSEPH. Simile

NURSE WILLISON. If you say so

JOSEPH. Am I here for my comfort
   Or for the comfort of the world?
   It seems my choices are the side show
   Or a waiting room for death

NURSE WILLISON. That sounds a bit dramatic

JOSEPH. Is there a cure for me?

NURSE WILLISON. You know that, Joseph
   They say you will go on just
   Becoming yourself
   Forever

Sixteen: Actress Visits

An actress has come to visit.

MRS HIGHFIELD. I am very grateful very grateful indeed
   Mr Merrick
   So very
   Honoured
   That you would pay me the compliment
   And spare me some of your time
   For what
   Must seem
   So trivial, so flighty a contrivance

JOSEPH. Time
   Is one of the things I have in abundance

MRS HIGHFIELD. You have a view at least
   And pleasant rooms

JOSEPH. I am plastic, Mrs Highfield
   I have no real shape
   So I arrange myself to fit the space I am given.
   I am intrigued
   Most who visit me

Come to gawp and excite their eyes
I imagine them in their townhouses
Whispering to Lady Whatever
'My dear
The ugliest face
The most revolting'
And so on
But you madam
Think I might be of use to you
I have never been to the theatre
I know nothing of that world
Although I have spent many a tedious hour
On a stage
What can this poor plastic
Breathing doll
Tell a lady of the limelight?

MRS HIGHFIELD. When people come to you
Nice ladies
Fine gentlemen
What do they want?

JOSEPH. I am told that in the poor districts
Just over these walls
Some children are permitted to touch the Queen
That they may be cured of their rashes and diseases
For the monarch's very touch
Has healing powers.
And contrariwise
The beautiful and the refined cross town to caress
Me
and perhaps a little of my beastliness
Will amend their relentless loveliness
Which sits like sugar in their dainty mouths.

MRS HIGHFIELD. An extraordinary observation

JOSEPH. Have *you* come to caress me?

MRS HIGHFIELD. Well here goes.
I have been engaged to play a role

At Fermalough's, on Fountain Court, off the Strand?
Fine house, acoustic a marvel
And Fermalough's a gem
Bit of a ladies' man of course
And cannot be told a thing
It *is* his company I suppose
Forgive me
I tend to waylay myself
Fermalough's have engaged your humble player
To realise a role in their forthcoming *Notre Dame de Paris*
Mr Tyrone will be playing Quasimodo
Do you know of him?
He's a bottler little Clarence
Oh stick to the script Lizzie
Forgive me Mr Merrick
The truth is
I am somewhat skittish
Perplexing eh
For one who spends her life under the greasepaint?

JOSEPH. You may ask of me
   What you wish
   Mrs Highfield
   I am The Elephant Man
   And you know what is said of elephants

MRS HIGHFIELD. They always remember?

JOSEPH. We have very thick skin

MRS HIGHFIELD. The role in which I have been cast
   Is that of Esmeralda
   You know the play?

JOSEPH. Remind me

MRS HIGHFIELD. It is a tale of romance
   And fantasy
   Set in the architecture
   Of an ancient city
   Esmeralda is a gypsy girl
   Vain

>   Proud
>   Powerful men desire her
>   And in one *coup de theatre*
>   She is about to be hanged

JOSEPH. Oh the poor girl

MRS HIGHFIELD. When Quasimodo comes
>   Swinging down on a rope
>   And carries Esmeralda up high to a bell tower
>   To keep her safe

JOSEPH. And is she safe?

MRS HIGHFIELD. For a time
>   But she cannot love Quasimodo
>   Even though he loves her

JOSEPH. Why not?

MRS HIGHFIELD. Quasimodo has a good heart but he is...

JOSEPH. French?

MRS HIGHFIELD. He is hunchbacked
>   And has a large wart above his eye

JOSEPH. I see

MRS HIGHFIELD. When Esmeralda is taken from death's door
>   She dies in a way
>   And ascends to a type of heaven
>   High in the bell tower
>   Perched over the roofs of Paris
>   She is meant to be the epitome
>   Of beauty
>   And allure
>   That I can do
>   But she inhabits this strange limbo
>   This place between one death and another
>   With her antithesis
>   Male
>   Grotesque
>   A brute

But tender hearted
They are brother and sister
Symbiosis
Celestial twins
In order to grasp Esmeralda
I need to grasp
That different thing she sometimes glimpses in the mirror

JOSEPH. My role is to be
Your
Different Thing

MRS HIGHFIELD. For this little piece of theatre's purposes
Yes

JOSEPH. Something that is human
And can never be

MRS HIGHFIELD. If you like

JOSEPH. Do you think it is possible to be both human
And something else?

MRS HIGHFIELD. Perhaps in the world of the imagination

JOSEPH. And that is the world I live in
I think it is possible to be human and monster
I think it is possible to change from human to Different Thing
And to move from different to human
I believe one might have all the accoutrements of humanity
But for the mind to be utterly inhuman within
And I also conceive
Of a mind and heart that is utterly human
But a form that is repulsive and laughable

MRS HIGHFIELD. I see

She doesn't.

I was rather hoping –
It seems ill-advised now
Here
Before you.

(*Suddenly.*) I did not really come
Because of the play.
I am considered by some poor deluded fools
Something of a beauty
But I have this fear
This nightmare
That one day
I shall stride out on the boards
And that they will not see all that and only see the
monstrosity that is the actual me and is trapped within and
I thought or formed a fancy as it were that you who I have
heard is something of a saint of holy figure trapped within
monstrosity might...

JOSEPH. I have no choice
I am not some crustacean
Which can move from shell to shell
This is my self
And I have nowhere else to live.
Can you leave your body, Mrs Highfield?

MRS HIGHFIELD. No

JOSEPH. How do you know?

MRS HIGHFIELD. It is impossible for a person to
That is to say
The mind
It only can exist inside oneself

JOSEPH. Yes inside yourself
I cannot speak for you
But I can tell you what it is to be me
My body is not
Predictable
It is what it is today
But tomorrow it may become
Something else
It goes where the spirit takes it
I and my head grow
Outwards ever outwards

On and on into infinity
Like the reverberations
Of a great bell.
What happens to Esmeralda?

MRS HIGHFIELD. Oh they get her
In the end

JOSEPH. I am sorry
And Quasimodo?

MRS HIGHFIELD. He dies
Of starvation
Clutching Esmeralda's dead body
And years later
Their bones are found
Entwined
In the embrace
They can never have
When living.

JOSEPH. The world of the imagination

JOSEPH *laughs and laughs*.

Seventeen: Learning to Dance

Another NURSE *and* JOSEPH.

NURSE GLYNDON. Oh it were quite wonderful
But it were very sad
There was this captain of the army, he was most dashing
And you could tell that Esmeralda she fancied him rotten
She was good your friend Mrs Highfield
For she just tossed her hair back, this big mane of jet black locks

JOSEPH. But Mrs Highfield has fair hair

NURSE GLYNDON. Ooh no not in this one she has gypsy hair doesn't she?

JOSEPH. That must be confusing

NURSE GLYNDON. And she danced like a gypsy and her
skirts were all flaring out
It gave us a good idea it did for –

JOSEPH. For what?

NURSE GLYNDON. Oh nothing.
Oh it were sad though at the end the sextons they opened up the tomb
And the bones of Esmeralda and the bones of Queasymodo
Just crumbled to dirt but their ghosts were together you see?
Oh I clapped and clapped I did
Til I thought my hands would fall off

JOSEPH. What did it give you an idea for?

NURSE GLYNDON. Sorry?

JOSEPH. What did it give you an idea for?

NURSE GLYNDON. No it's nothing I just thought
That it would be a right lark
To dress as Esmeralda
For this ball
The hospital ball
Mr Frederick Treves he's that famous surgeon
What writes about you

JOSEPH. I don't remember him

NURSE GLYNDON. Well he's throwing us all a fancy dress ball a Christmas fancy dress ball a ball

JOSEPH. Fancy dress is…

NURSE GLYNDON. It's when you wear clothes like someone famous or something and everyone chooses something and then they come to the ball
And to tell the truth I have never been to a ball
But I believe there are shining fancy lights and
Great bowls of punch and a band in ever so smart uniforms
They play and everything shines and even though everyone

    is all dressed up
    In make believe they
    Dance and twirl about the room

JOSEPH. I had no idea you could dance, Nurse Glyndon

NURSE GLYNDON. Ooh I can give it a go.
    Here
    You stand like this
    And you put your claw there
    Sorry
    Joke
    And no don't look at me
    You look over there

JOSEPH. Why?

NURSE GLYNDON. Cos that's how it's done
    Hold onto me I won't break
    And then you just move your good foot when I go
    Ready?
    Da da dada
    Da da
    Da da da da da da
    Well, it's a start
    Again
    Da da Da da
    Ooohh look at Joseph
    You can quite cut the floor up
    Da Da da
    Da da

JOSEPH. It is most tiring
    But there is a crisis, nurse
    What fancy dress shall I wear?

NURSE GLYNDON. Joseph
    This is what I was trying to not say
    It isn't a ball for patients
    It's for the staff
    For the orderlies and nurses and all
    For us
    It's not for you

JOSEPH. Oh.
Oh.
Maybe I shall listen
In my room

NURSE GLYNDON. There's a good man

She leaves, humming, dancing.

JOSEPH (*sarcastically to himself*). Maybe I shall listen in my room.

Eighteen: Dead Body

JOSEPH *sleeping. Strange sounds, someone fighting for air... or is it sexual? He wakes, listens for a while. He gets up, takes his stick, starts walking; the sound gets louder as he nears. He walks in on a porter preparing the dead body of* MISS FORDHAM.

MORGUE PORTER. You really shouldn't be here.

JOSEPH. Was she in pain?

MORGUE PORTER. Pain? Oh yes, she was in pain alright, at the end there. It's normal. That's the normal state for when you're leaving the world.

JOSEPH. Like it's raining

MORGUE PORTER. What're you saying, it's boiling out there. That's why I've got to get on with this.
Got to move fast in the heat. The flesh turns so quick I tell you.

JOSEPH. The water. For washing. Like rain. A rainy day.

MORGUE PORTER. If you say so. Here you want to help?

JOSEPH *shakes his head.*

One minute you're here and then one minute you're not. Shooting stars aren't we?

JOSEPH. You are a philosopher

MORGUE PORTER. I touch the dead, don't I? Lends itself to a certain… reflectiveness.

JOSEPH (*gesturing*). What will you do with her?

MORGUE PORTER. This one? See, the skull's interesting. And what those last few weeks did to her spine. The world needs this sort of stuff, for museums and libraries and, you know, to educate. So, it's her bones I'm interested in.

She carries the body of MISS FORDHAM *into the mist. Dance music rises and swirls.*

Nineteen: Outside the Ball

Music of the ball. Golden light from upstage.

JOSEPH *watches, then nears.*

A NURSE *comes out, in a Cyclops costume.*

CYCLOPS NURSE. Joseph
  What on earth are you doing up here?
  You know it is forbidden
  For you to leave the confines of the courtyard and your rooms

JOSEPH. I thought I might just –

CYCLOPS NURSE. You thought what?
  You might dance
  Joseph?
  I appreciate this institution
  Can feel peculiar
  Removed from reality
  But you must understand
  This is a place for the sick
  The ill

Those who have something wrong with them
If we permitted patients –

JOSEPH. There is nothing wrong with me

CYCLOPS NURSE. Joseph
Your very body belies that claim

A NURSE dressed as a mermaid and NURSE WILLISON, dressed as Quasimodo, enter.

MERMAID NURSE. Oh it's so bloomin hot in there!
Mr Merrick
What are you doing here? What if the big gentlemen see you? You have to vanish now.

NURSE WILLISON. Joseph
What if people
Saw you?

JOSEPH. I thought they might like to see their prize specimen
But maybe I am already here

JOSEPH goes up to the QUASIMODO NURSE. He prods the hump with his stick. He touches the lump on the NURSE's face, grasps it, pulls off the whole mask.

I will never understand the rules
You measure me, scrape at me
You wash me like a dirty dish
You fill my days with trifles
You talk at me
And congratulate yourselves
You are being so kind
I am the most extraordinary thing in this massive city
And yet when you look at me
You cannot see me
What is this place
What are the rules
What am I
A statue on a plinth
A stuffed ape in a glass case
All your wounds and diseases

Kneaded together like bread dough
What?

NURSE WILLISON. Come on Joseph
It is just a costume
Just pretend
From a popular play
It is theatre
No need to
Get upset
No need to make a spectacle of yourself

JOSEPH. You made a spectacle of me
You are all monsters
All of you
You are all monsters

JOSEPH *lumbers out.*

The MERMAID-NURSE *throws her hands in the air.*

MERMAID NURSE. Oh bleeding heck.

Enter MATRON, *dressed as Medusa*

MATRON. What's the commotion?

CYCLOPS NURSE. It's Mr Merrick ma'am
He's gone.

MATRON. Gone?

NURSE WILLISON. Onto Whitechapel Road

MATRON. Oh Lord. Alone?

MATRON *and the* NURSES *rush in pursuit.*

Twenty: Snow Man

It is snowing.

JOSEPH *in awe, as if in a cathedral. He speaks softly, clearly, clearer than he has before.*

JOSEPH. Alone.
   Galaxies whirl
   And underneath
   The cold rock murmurs deep
   Deep until soundlessness smothers
   But here, alone in this little moment –
   The city
   All around me
   The whispers
   And the groans
   The hooves of horses on the cobblestones
   The dull hiss
   Of a thousand fires
   Bedded down for the night
   The creaking of window panes
   As the bricks and the mullions
   Contract
   The sweet hushing of rain –
   The city envelopes.
   I am mutating
   I am coming into my own
   A changing thing
   My senses
   Are not the senses of all of them
   The dwellers of the night
   The tramps
   The beggars
   The chimney sweeps
   The mad
   The troglodytes that spewed from the bowels of ships
   They are all one species
   And I see them

In the night
That species *homo sapiens*
I hear their snores
I smell their breath
My senses yes
They change, they bulge too
My eyes
See as no other being has seen
My ears
Pick up frequencies undocumented
My nose
Catches decay
And perfume
No other human knows

He stops by an elm.

Sap surges
Song of hope
Bark wrinkles, folds
Branches spread tendrils into air
I hear the tree
Sing
'*When I was a seed*
I had no idea
And I knew not what a tree must be'
And here
In the trunk
A termite's nest
Where white bulbs
Seethe and spill
The nest bubbles in wood
Eats away flesh
Is neither bad nor good
And here on the termites parasites dwell
Chewing into the insect-flesh
Laying miniscule eggs
Which promise to fizz and crack I see I hear I feel it all
This thing Nature
Has no true form

Is just an endless flow of pictures and light:
Fungus bulges from the dampness
Scales spread on the leaves
Ichneumon wasps erupt from the bellies of caterpillars
And everywhere, nature bleeds.

NURSES, *looking for* JOSEPH.

NURSES. Joseph!
Joseph!
Mr Merrick!

JOSEPH stands still. The NURSES *go right past him, keep looking through the theatre.*

The YOUNG MAN *enters.*

YOUNG MAN. You will catch your death out here.

JOSEPH. A trap

YOUNG MAN. Pardon me?

JOSEPH. A trap
I'm a trap
I'll catch death.

YOUNG MAN. And I'll catch you.

He offers JOSEPH *a drink of gin. We can still hear the* NURSES *looking for him in the distance.*

JOSEPH. I thought I wished to be like them
To be among them
But I cannot.
Do you know how species begin?

YOUNG MAN. What a peculiar question. How do species begin? Species are. It is a means of classifying. The Lord makes 'em and that's what they are.

JOSEPH. No
Not with me
A new species springs forth
By random fate

Or by a circus animal scaring a woman
Or because the dark city
Is changing, creating.

YOUNG MAN. And you are a new species I take it?

JOSEPH. I think I am
I am not a wrong version of them
I am not a man with a disease
I am not a freak
An error
To be kept in cage
I do not need a cure
I do not need to be protected
I am a new species
Sprung from the new nature
Of foundries
And locomotives
Of putrid air
And circuses
homo elephantidae
A species of One
That starts
And ends with me.

He topples over. The snow covers him until he is a pile of white.

The NURSES *gradually enter, still in their fancy dress. One comes forward.*

NURSE WILLISON. We should give him a decent burial

The YOUNG MAN *shakes his head.*

YOUNG MAN. No
I shall take it from here.

The End.

www.nickhernbooks.co.uk

facebook.com/nickhernbooks

twitter.com/nickhernbooks